LET THE KIDS PLAY

80 Exciting Soccer Training Sessions

by Andrew Donnery

**Library of Congress
Cataloging - in - Publication Data**

by Andrew Donnery
LET THE KIDS PLAY

ISBN No. 1-59164-088-1
Lib. of Congress Control No. 2004096673
© 2004

*Art Direction, Editing and
Layout*
Bryan R. Beaver

Cover Photo
Richard Kentwell

Printed by
DATA REPRODUCTIONS
Auburn, Michigan

Reedswain Publishing
562 Ridge Road
Spring City, PA 19475
800.331.5191
www.reedswain.com
info@reedswain.com

CONTENTS

Introduction

After years of coaching and reading other coaching books I decided to write my own. I have been involved with soccer for over 25 years and have been involved at the school, club, college and professional level. I also have a background in psychology which enables me to look at soccer training from a different (more child centered and development oriented) angle.

I currently work as director of youth development at a soccer club with 4000 players and run summer camps with another several thousand players, and what started off as a request for me to give ideas for training sessions gave way to the creation of an in depth manual of drills and exercises to be used by my staff of 200 or so coaches.

During my research for this book I discovered an alarming fact; there is an enormous drop in people playing soccer when they get to their teens. Consider that in the USA 17 million people play soccer, 80% of this population is between 6 and 11 years old and 6 out of 10 kids between 5 and 9 years old will have soccer as their first option as a sport. Then consider that by age 14, 70% of these players have dropped out of the game. (Statistics from fifa.com)

While there are many reasons for this drop off I believe a contributing factor is the philosophy of coaching held by many youth coaches. The fact that many coaches view winning, and winning at all costs, above player development, in my view leads to the dissatisfaction of many of the players on the field. I have lost count of the number of games I've watched where the coach has put the biggest kid at the back (the one the parents refer to as the one with the "big foot") and then the fastest kid in attack. The coach then tells the kid at the back to kick it as far as possible up the field for the other kid to chase. Then the kid receives positive reinforcement when he launches it downfield and hears the parents scream "yeah, great play, wow, big foot". The young player believes this is the way to play soccer. The coach may well get a win out of this method of play, but is it really a job well done?

What one has to ask is how many times did the other players in the team touch the ball? Where is the fun in this type of game, a game in which you run up and down the field and never touch the ball? Even when some players touch the ball and they make a mistake, parents can be heard making negative comments on the line, comments that are often repeated by the player's own team mates. Where does this all end? The player may even quit the game because he or she is so embarrassed.

I encourage coaches to teach teamwork, leadership, patience, commitment, and respect among others. We need to make the whole team good; it is not good enough to be a part of a team that wins because two forwards score all the goals and get all the praise.

Coach educators need to focus on becoming knowledgeable in order to enable every player on the team to contribute to the game; young players need to be allowed to experiment with the game, to figure out for themselves what does and doesn't work. The result will be a successful team whose players can enjoy the sport of soccer. Soccer is not a pigeon holed sport where coaches give out set plays and shout plays from the sideline. It is a game that changes from minute to minute and needs players that have been coached to deal with this demand.

The training sessions in this book have been created to encour-age players to think, to enable them to process information and to find solutions. Players in practice sessions should be touching the ball as much as possible and performing game related drills and this book is full of ideas for coaches to use. The following sessions are set up in a way that provides an environment that the kids will respond to and learn from.
As coaches we need to constantly evaluate what we do and how we do it. This book will help to introduce you to a new way of thinking and coaching.

Hopefully you will find the sessions helpful.

Let the kids think for themselves and most of all let them have fun and play!

Coaching Soccer

There are three things you need to contemplate before setting up your soccer session.

1)   The epuipment to which you have access.
2)   The number of players.
3)   The practice area.

Many of the sessions listed in this book are set up using a 10x10 yard grid (see below).

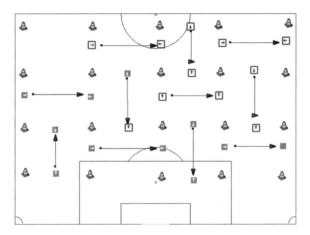

Doing it this way allows the coach to set up the session in an organized fashion, utilize the space and make the drill work. The way the players are setup in the drill helps keep the players' minds on what they are doing. This way, you can quickly change your session from a 10x10 to a 20x20 or 30x30. The less cones you have to move during the session the better your session will flow (players get bored waiting around if you have to change your session). The sessions listed in this book provide you with measurements and an outline of the drill, if at any time the drill needs modifying or isn't working, change it. As a coach, never stand by and let the session fail if you feel you can make the session better by modifying it.

All of the sessions listed in this book are tried and tested and are provided because they will work and are easy to understand.

Coaching players

Keep your players interested, if they are not. they will resist change or any new ideas you present. They must be enthusiastic, a player who is, is willing to try new things and learn. As a coach you need to set good standards and should show good demonstrations (if you can't demo a session yourself, find someone who can or get one of the kids to show you). Many players learn from watching other players, encourage them to watch soccer on TV or go to live matches. This is an invaluable learning tool. By watching their heroes and people they admire they will strive to succeed and have the motivation needed to excel in soccer.

Motivation

Encourage and motivate the players. The players should want to be at practice and enjoy it and not look on it as a chore. You will be amazed how easy it is to coach players who are enjoying themselves.

Preparation

Plan your session on paper before you go to the field. Does it make sense? Does it flow? Will the players understand it? Do you know what you are coaching? Check all equipment before you get to the field. Are the balls pumped? Are the goals safe? Are any of the players wearing jewelry? Is the field safe? If you are doing a heading exercise and the players are younger, don't pump the balls up too hard.

Preparation is the key when it comes to coaching a session.

Key Factors

The sessions are put together in such a way that the players will receive constant repetitions in each drill rather than listening to a wordy explanation from the coach. You can list the important key factors beforehand and then let the kids play and find the rest out for themselves.

4

Remember, for your players *practice makes permanence.*

Simple to complex

The early sessions in each chapter start off in a simplistic manner and become more challenging. The players will have little trouble understanding the drills. If you look closely at the sessions you will realize they have little or no stoppages and everyone is involved in continuous action. Never start off with an 8 v 8 and then go to a 1 v 1. You can use the following numbers as a guideline for your session 1v1, 2v1, 3v2, 4v4, 8v8 etc. If you start with an 11v11 you may struggle to the get the meaning of your session across to the players. Build up slowly and show it in a simple way before you go to a complex situation.

Progression

By adding or removing players in the drills you can give either team a numerical advantage to aid the drill. (this will help if the players are of different ages or abilities).

- Change the rules, let different players have different rules (this can help those of less abilities)
- Add/Subtract players (this will help teams become balanced or overloaded)
- Change the size of the area (smaller area if they are better players, bigger area if they are players with lesser ability)

Stopping the session

If you see something wrong in the session you need to stop it. You can have a signal, a whistle, or shout "stop" or "freeze". Make the players aware of the signal beforehand and what it means. If you are working on crossing and finishing and the attackers make poor runs, you need to coach it. Try not to stop the session too much. If you do, the players will become restless and bored.

Paint the picture, show me and get out.

If you stop the session, what are you going to do? Do the players understand why you stopped it? Using the example above (crossing and finishing), the attacker makes a poor run and you shout "freeze". Walk through the movement you would like to see the attacker do, then get him to show you (this will answer the question "does he understand?") and then get out (restart the session just before you stopped it). This way the players get to rehearse what you have just explained.

Functional Practices

A functional practice involves one or more players developing their playing role (function) in realistic situations and appropriate areas.

- Phase of Play
A fully opposed practice involving all attacking and defending players who are regarded as primary and secondary considerations designed to improve performance and understanding around a chosen attacking or defending theme located in an appropriate area of the field.

- Small Sided Games
A free flowing game involving two equal teams with less than eleven players: 6v6, 8v8, 9v9 with goalkeepers.

- Full Sized Games
Use full sized games to 'cement' an understanding of functions and roles in team play as an individual, as a unit or as a team.

Coaching match conditions

A condition can be introduced to any session to aid concentration on a particular aspect of play. If I wanted to work on moving the ball quickly I could limit the players to playing one touch. This would create a false environment for the players but it would encourage the players to pass and move the ball quickly. Only work with these restrictions for 15-20 mins.

Ending the session

I always finish with a game or a competition. 8 v 8 (or how many players you have max 11 v 11) with everyone involved. After all, the kids come to soccer practice to play. *Let them play and score goals.*

Cool Down

An important end to every session and game. The players' bodies for the last few hours have been running at a high intensity and need to be cooled down. Research has proven when players "cool down" they are less likely to suffer from strains and stiffness.

Make the players do any of the following:

⊕ Skip
⊕ Jog
⊕ Swing their arms as they skip and jog
⊕ Longer stretches
⊕ Limb stretching
⊕ Take on fluids
⊕ Lie on your back and shake your legs in the air
⊕ Put on extra clothing

Warm up and Stretching

One of the major problems about coaching youth teams is the players turn up ready to play and shoot. They arrive at the field and immediately start to shoot at the goal. One of your first jobs as a coach is to make the players understand why it is important for them to warm up.

Why should you warm up?

The body and muscles are not ready to compete at the intensity the soccer game brings. For example, you don't jump into your car on a cold frosty morning and go racing down the street at 100 mph. Your car (like the soccer player) needs time to warm up.

During the warm up your pulse rate quickens and blood flow increases, making more nutrients and oxygen available to your muscles. Also, your body temperature increases and enables the muscles' movement.

From a psychological standpoint it gets the players ready for the game. They are touching the ball and preparing their minds for the game.

If the players don't warm up properly they run the risk of injury.

Your warm ups will change depending upon if it is a game or a training session. The chapters in this book start with simple sessions which would be suitable to use as warm ups. If you are planning a session on passing, lead into that session with a warm up passing drill.

Passing & Control

Passing and control are the two most important techniques required to play soccer. When you watch the best teams in the world play they are all expert passers and can control the ball with ease.

The important key factors to remember when doing a passion session are accuracy, weight, disguise and timing. If you know the key factors you can coach the session. The important key factors to remember when doing a control session are getting in line with the ball, the choice of control surfaces; relax when the ball comes and deciding what type of pass you are going to do and how you are going to execute it.

The passing technique needs to be broken into the following: correct technique when using a pass, the range of techniques and when to use those techniques. There is no better way to win a game than to pass the opponent into submission.

The following chapter will introduce you to passing and control sessions.

TRAINING SESSION 1:
Improving Passing in Teams of 5

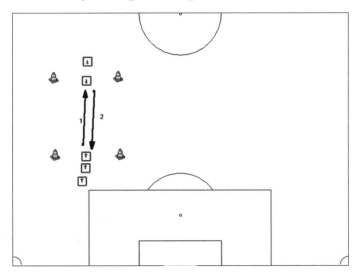

Setup

- Boxes 10 x 10 yds.
- 3 Players on one side with a ball and two on the other side
- 1st pass is played to the other side, then the passer follows his pass and joins the back of the opposite line.
- The player who receives the ball passes it back and follows the ball
- Ball is not allowed to leave the box
- 10 passes can be a goal
- Make the area bigger if players have trouble
- Change the style of pass (inside, outside etc.)
- Keep the ball moving

Coaching Points

- Accuracy of the pass
- Weight of the pass

TRAINING SESSION 2:
Warm Up for a Practice Session to Improve 1-2

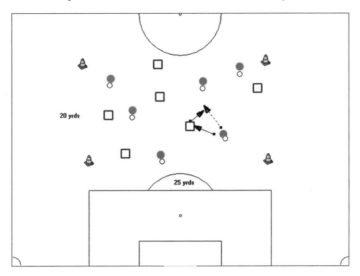

Setup

⊕ 25 x 20 yds
⊕ 6 white, 6 gray
⊕ Players with the ball pass then move into space ready to receive the ball.
⊕ Keep the players moving , swap roles after 3 mins
⊕ Play for about 10 - 15 mins

Coaching Points

⊕ Accuracy of the pass
⊕ Weight of the pass
⊕ Are they talking?
⊕ Are they moving into space?

TRAINING SESSION 3:
Improve Control and Passing with the Triangle Game

Setup

- ⊕ 2 players with one ball by a coned triangle.
- ⊕ Gray player passes the ball to the white player, who controls the ball with the inside of the foot to the outside of the cone and passes it back.
- ⊕ Gray player stays on the cone and the pass has to be through the coned area.
- ⊕ Play for about 5-10 minutes.
- ⊕ Work on all types of control surfaces (inside, outside, laces), then work on all types of passes (inside, outside, laces)

Coaching Points

- ⊕ Accuracy and weight of the passes
- ⊕ Make sure the players concentrate and keep the ball under control at all times.
- ⊕ Body position when they receive and when they pass

Variations
- ⊕ Right, left foot.
- ⊕ The players can throw the ball and use different parts of the body to control
- ⊕ Mix it up, right foot receive, left foot pass

TRAINING SESSION 4:
Improving Control 5v2

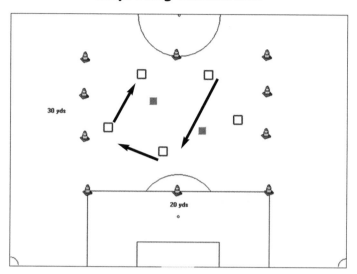

Setup

⊛ 20 x 30 yds
⊛ The white team tries to keep possession of the ball
⊛ The two gray players try to get the ball

Coaching Points

⊛ Accuracy, weight, disguise & timing of the passes
⊛ Control the ball to the safe side.
⊛ What part of the body receives the ball?
⊛ Pick your pass.
⊛ Don't pass to players who have no options.

Variation

⊛ Change the area if the players struggle (make it bigger)
⊛ Fewer players (if they struggle) or more players (if they do it well)
⊛ Communication

TRAINING SESSION 5:
Movement Off the Ball - 3v2 in 2 Areas

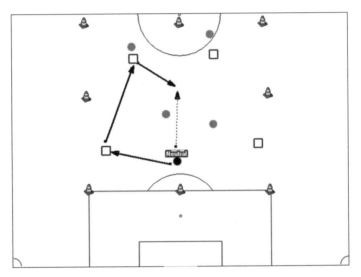

Setup

- ☺ 20 x 30
- ☺ 2 reds/2 blues and a green neutral player
- ☺ Neutral player plays in both areas and for the team who has possession
- ☺ Players are not allowed to go into the other area (except for the neutral player)
- ☺ 10 passes = one goal - If the other team wins the ball they try to keep possession.
- ☺ 5 passes before they can change areas (less passes if it is too difficult)

Coaching Points

- ☺ Accuracy, Weight, Disguise & Timing of the passes
- ☺ Movement off the ball
- ☺ Space created, ball delivered, man arrives
- ☺ Communication

TRAINING SESSION 6:
Improving Support - 3v3 + 2 Neutral Players

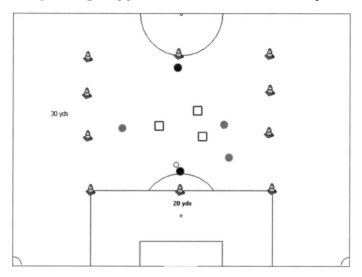

Setup

- 20 x 30 yds
- Possession, keep the ball 3 v3 using 2 neutral players
- Limit number of touches (1, 2, 3), then open up play.
- Add restrictions on touches

Coaching Points

- Accuracy, Weight, Disguise & Timing of the passes
- What type of pass?
- Only play when you can support the player.
- Don't watch your pass.
- Movement off the ball
- Communication
- Play the ball to the safe side of the man.
- Move to the side and check.
- Create space before you receive the ball.

TRAINING SESSION 7:
Scoring with a Pass - 4v4

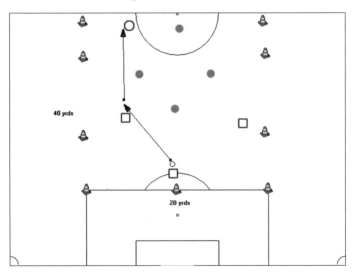

Setup

- ⚽ 20 x 40 yds
- ⚽ 4 Grays, 4 Whites
- ⚽ Score a goal by releasing one of your players into the opponent's area (final 10 yd boxes)
- ⚽ No dribbling, make them pass and move.

Coaching Points

- ⚽ Accuracy, Weight, Disguise & Timing of the passes
- ⚽ Movement off the ball
- ⚽ Communication

TRAINING SESSION 8:
Scoring After a Pass and a Run - 4v4

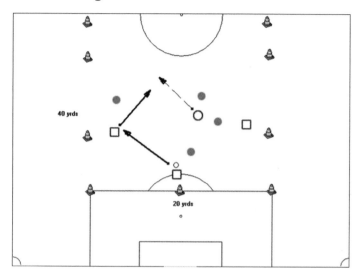

Setup

- ✪ 20 x 40
- ✪ Similar to the previous exercise - Two teams of four players
- ✪ Score a goal by making your player get into the opponent's final 10 yard area
- ✪ You can only score if there are no attackers in the opponent's area when you play the ball.
- ✪ No dribbling, pass only

Coaching Points

- ✪ Accuracy, Weight, Disguise & Timing of the passes
- ✪ Coach movement off the ball
- ✪ Communication

TRAINING SESSION 9:
Improving Passing and Movement - 5v5

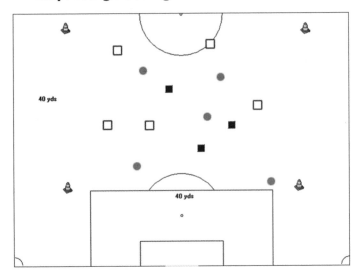

40 yds

40 yds

Setup

⚽ 40 x 40
⚽ 5 v 5 match
⚽ 3 black players join in with the team in possession
⚽ Goal scored by getting the ball over the opponent's end line (white top, gray bottom)
⚽ 10 minute games

Coaching Points

⚽ Make them play one touch, pass and move.
⚽ When to play and when to pass, beat the opponent on your own or with a 1-2 combination
⚽ Watch the passing
⚽ Movement after the pass?

Heading

Writing this introduction for heading started me thinking of all the memorable headed goals I had seen. Strikingly, the header I remember most was a header from Pele which was saved (so that doesn't count). Pele leaped to get a cross, headed it downwards and somehow Gordan Banks clawed it up off the floor and over the bar (so thanks to Gordon Banks I can't use that as an example). Thinking further I remember Miroslav Klose of Germany in the 2002 World Cup finals scoring 5 headed goals.

Even though it is a hard technique to master it can prove an invaluable tool.

Important key factors to remember when coaching heading are the part of the head to use (forehead), keeping your eyes open and correct body position when heading (standing square to your partner).
At times this can be a difficult technique to coach, hopefully the following sessions will help.

The following chapter will introduce you to heading.

TRAINING SESSION 10:
Heading Warm Up 1

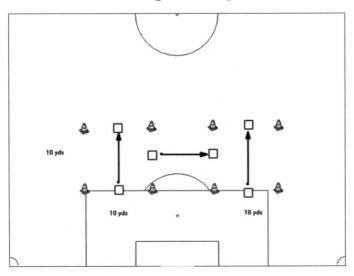

Setup

⚽ 10 x 10
⚽ 2 players in each box
⚽ Players throw the ball to their partners, who head it back

Coaching Points

⚽ Part of the head (forehead)
⚽ Eyes open
⚽ Body position when heading (standing square to your partner)

TRAINING SESSION 11:
Heading Warm Up 2

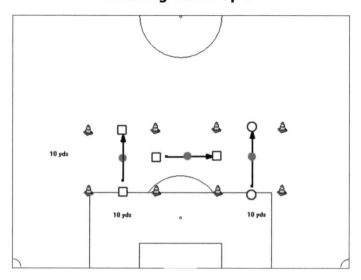

Setup

- ⊛ 10 x 10
- ⊛ 2 players in each box with a defender in the middle
- ⊛ Players throw the ball to their partners over the defender and the partners head it back over the defender

Coaching Points

- ⊛ Part of the head (forehead)
- ⊛ Eyes open
- ⊛ Body position when heading (standing square to your partner)

TRAINING SESSION 12:
Heading Warm Up 3

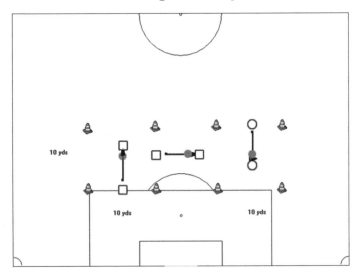

Setup

- ❁ 10 x 10
- ❁ 2 players in each box with a defender in the middle
- ❁ Players throw the ball to their partner over the defender and the partners head it back over the defender
- ❁ Have the attacker stand close behind the defender. The attacker has to judge when to jump to head the ball

Coaching Points

- ❁ Part of the head (forehead)
- ❁ Eyes open
- ❁ Body position when heading (standing square to your partner)

Variation

- ❁ Get the defender to jump just before the player throws the ball.

TRAINING SESSION 13:
Heading Warm Up 4

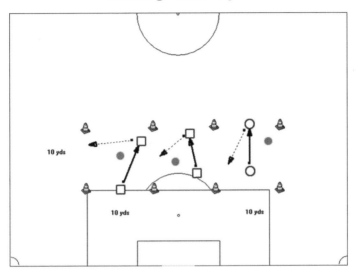

Setup

- 10 x 10
- 2 players in each box with a defender in the middle
- Players throw the ball to their partners, who head it back
- The attackers now move around the box creating space
- The player with the ball is not allowed to move with the ball in his hands
- The defender tries to stop the ball with his head only
- 5-10 mins

Coaching Points

- Part of the head (forehead)
- Eyes open
- Body position when heading may now be side-on or facing
- Movement off the ball

TRAINING SESSION 14:
Heading in a Circle

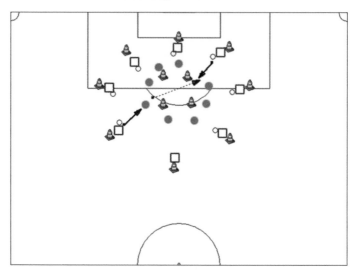

Setup

- Circle of cones with a gate in the middle (size depending upon number of players)
- 8 outside and 8 inside
- Players on the outside have the ball and throw the ball to the players on the inside
- Once they head it back the players in the middle have to go through the gate and receive the ball from another outside player
- 5-10 mins then switch outside for inside

Coaching Points

- Part of the head (forehead)
- Eyes open
- Body position when heading may now be side-on or facing

TRAINING SESSION 15:
Heading Game with 2 Full Size Goals

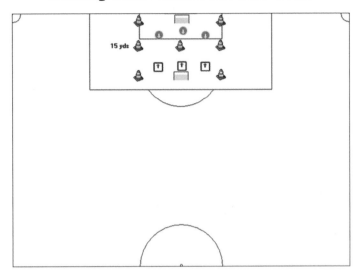

Setup

⊕ Width of the 6 yd box x 15 yds
⊕ 3 players in each area
⊕ Players throw the ball to their partners who try to score with a header.
⊕ Players have to be on their goal line when they try to score.
⊕ The defender tries to stop the ball with his head only.
⊕ 5-10 mins

Coaching Points

⊕ Part of the head (forehead)
⊕ Eyes open
⊕ Body position when heading may now be side on or facing
⊕ Attacking headers (down) and defensive headers (up and out)

Variations

⊕ Add more players
⊕ Make the area larger

TRAINING SESSION 16:
Heading from 3 Servers

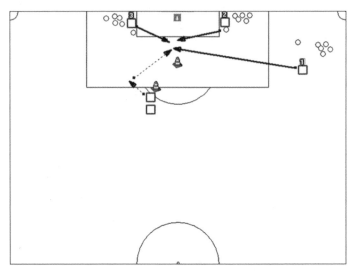

Setup

- ✪ 3 servers, attackers and a goalkeeper
- ✪ Players receive the ball from the servers and have to score with a header
- ✪ Server 1 delivers the ball with his feet, servers 2 and 3 throw the ball
- ✪ 5-10 mins

Coaching Points

- ✪ Part of the head (forehead)
- ✪ Eyes open
- ✪ Body position when heading may now be side-on or facing
- ✪ Attacking headers (down) and defensive headers (up and out)
- ✪ Movement of the attackers
- ✪ Where is the keeper?

Variations

- ✪ Add defenders
- ✪ Switch sides

TRAINING SESSION 17:
Heading from Servers 6v6

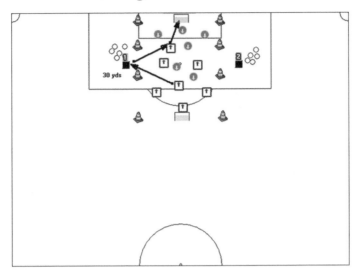

Setup

- Width of the 6 yd box x 30 yds
- 6 v 6 players
- Players throw the ball to the server (1 & 2) and try to score from the return
- Servers can move up and down the cone line
- Goals can only be scored with headers
- As soon as the ball hits the ground they pick it up and throw it to the server
- 5-10 mins

Coaching Points

- Part of the head (forehead)
- Eyes open
- Body position when heading may now be side-on or facing
- Attacking headers (down) and defensive headers (up and out)
- Movement

TRAINING SESSION 18:
Headball Game

Setup

- 40 x 40 yds
- 6 v 6 players
- Start the game from the keepers.
- First pass has to be a throw, from the throw you have to head it to a teammate or to the goal.
- The passing progression will be 1) throw 2) head 3) throw.
- You are not allowed to throw it into the goal.

Coaching Points

- Part of the head (forehead)
- Eyes open
- Body position when heading may now be side-on or facing.
- Attacking headers (down) and defensive headers (up and out)
- Movement

Heading Runway Game

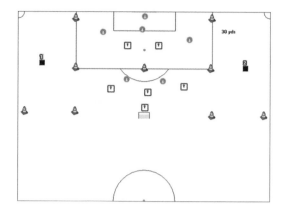

Setup

⊛ 30 yds long and width of field with runways up to the edge of the penalty box
⊛ 6 v 6 with 2 servers
⊛ Players pass the ball to the server (1 & 2) and try to score from the return
⊛ Servers can move up and down the cone line
⊛ Players only score with their heads
⊛ Players are not allowed to leave their area
⊛ 3 plus keeper v 2 in each area in favor of the defenders
⊛ 5-10 mins

Coaching Points

⊛ Part of the head (forehead)
⊛ Eyes open
⊛ Body position when heading may now be side-on or facing
⊛ Attacking headers (down) and defensive headers (up and out)
⊛ Movement
⊛ Encourage early crosses

Variation

⊛ Add free players who can go anywhere and/or players have no restrictions
⊛ Add other players in the runways (1v1, 2v1 or 2v2 etc)

Dribbling & Turning

The thrill and excitement of watching Diego Maradona weave through the England defense in the 1986 World Cup is a memory that I will never forget. Watching this soccer genius pick the ball up on the half way line and beat man after man left me breathless. Our fascination with watching the world's best dribblers continues and will never cease. Dribbling past opponents is a technique which needs to be coached and encouraged. Our soccer world needs exciting players who can dribble, let's encourage that.

The key factors for dribbling are confidence, close control in the approach, feinting & accelerating away.

The following chapter will introduce you to how to set up dribbling and turning sessions.

TRAINING SESSION 20:
Individual Turning #1 - 10 x 10

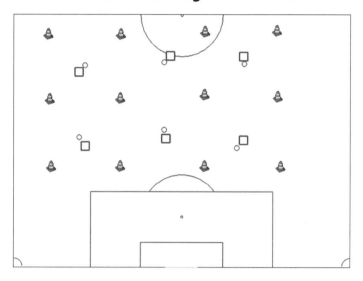

Setup

- ☻ 10 x 10 yd boxes
- ☻ Great for a warm up; everyone has a ball and his own square
- ☻ Show them a simple turn (Cruyff, hook, drag back, pull back)
- ☻ 15-20 mins
- ☻ Easy session to work on various turns

Coaching Points

- ☻ Head up, watch the players.
- ☻ Work on technique.
- ☻ Slowly to begin, get it right then speed up

TRAINING SESSION 21:
Individual Turning #2 - 10 x 10

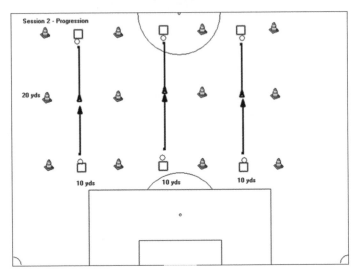

Setup

- 10 x 20 yds
- Similar to setup to #1, everyone has a ball and now they share the space with their partner.
- Run at your partner and just before you reach each other do a simple turn (Cruyff, hook, drag back, pull back), then jog back to your start position.
- 15-20 mins

Coaching Points

- Head up (otherwise you will bump into each other), watch the players.
- Work on technique.
- Slowly to begin, get it right then speed up

TRAINING SESSION 22:
Individual Turning #3 - 30 x 20

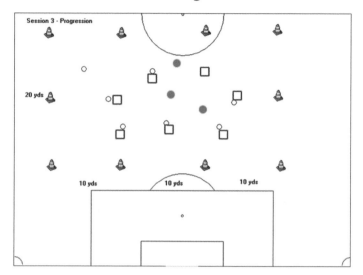

Setup

- ☺ 30 x 20 yds.
- ☺ Everyone has a ball except for 3 players (Gray).
- ☺ Start to move around the area, when you shout go, the Gray team try to tackle the White team and knock the ball out of the area.
- ☺ Encourage the players to do the turns you went through earlier (hook, drag back, pull back, Cruyff etc).

Coaching Points

- ☺ The players should be aware of what is around them, when they should do what turn.
- ☺ Work on technique.
- ☺ Slowly to begin, get it right then speed up.
- ☺ Accelerate out of the turn.

TRAINING SESSION 23:
Turning Tag Game

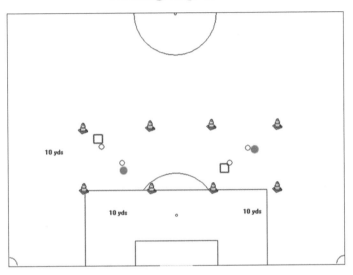

Setup

- 10 x 10 yds.
- Everyone has a ball, 2 in each box.
- Grays try to knock the white ball out while keeping control of their own ball
- Encourage the players to do the turns to avoid being tagged

Coaching Points

- Players should be aware of what is around them, when they should do what turn.
- Work on technique.
- Slowly to begin, get it right then speed up.
- Accelerate out of the turn.

TRAINING SESSION 24:
Improving Turning and Dribbling

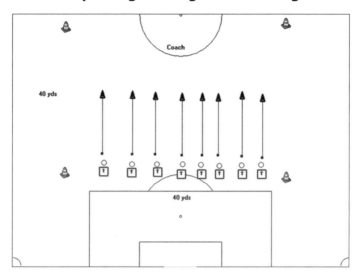

Setup

⊙ 40 x 40
⊙ 8 players, great for younger age groups
⊙ Dribble towards the coach.
⊙ Coach shouts a turn (Cruyff,drag back etc)

Coaching Points

⊙ Execute the technique, accelerate away.

TRAINING SESSION 25:
Improve Control and Turning in a Circle

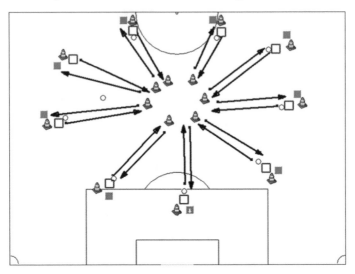

Setup

- Half Field (depends upon number of players)
- 2 players at each outside cone (1 gray, 1 white).
- White players jog to the inner circle, perform a turn close to the inner circle, jog back to the starting position and pass the ball to the gray players.
- Do a variety of turns.
- This setup works best when you have large numbers.

Coaching Points

- Control
- Execute the turn
- Accelerate away

TRAINING SESSION 26:
Improve Controlling and Turning with an Opponent Behind

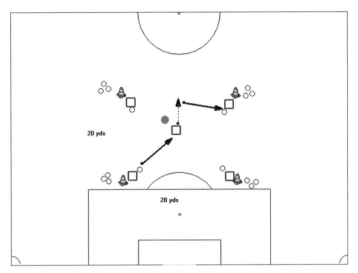

Setup

- ⊛ 20 x 20
- ⊛ 4 white players on the outside, 1 white/1 gray inside the square.
- ⊛ White is the attacker, white players on the outside play the ball to the white player in the middle
- ⊛ If the gray player gets the ball he becomes the attacker.
- ⊛ Work for 2-3 minutes, then switch

Coaching Points

- ⊛ Good control, good turn and be aware of what is around you
- ⊛ Where is the defender?

Variation

- ⊛ Smaller area
- ⊛ Limit the touches
- ⊛ Require more than one touch

TRAINING SESSION 27:
Improve Controlling and Turning with an Opponent Behind #2

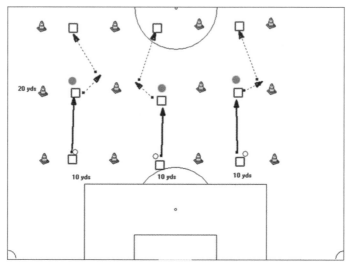

Setup

- ⚽ 10 x 20
- ⚽ 9 players (6 white, 3 gray)
- ⚽ Whites attack, the idea is for the white player in the middle to get the ball from the player at the bottom
- ⚽ If a gray player gets the ball he becomes the attacker.
- ⚽ Work for 2-3 minutes, then change players.

Coaching Points

- ⚽ Good control, good turn and be aware of what is around.
- ⚽ Where is the defender?

Variation

- ⚽ Limit the touches
- ⚽ Require more than one touch

TRAINING SESSION 28:
Turning Game

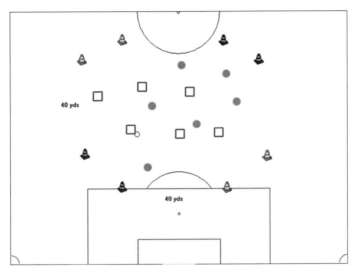

Setup

- 40 x 40 yds
- 6 v 6
- Gray team tries to score in white's goal.
- White team scores in gray's goal

Coaching Points

- Emphasize turning and control.
- Be aware of what is around.
- Encourage the players to do a turn when they can.
- By having two goals you are encouraging the players to turn.

TRAINING SESSION 29:
6 v 5 Turning Match

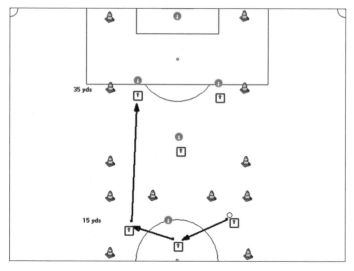

Setup

- 30 x 50 yds
- 6 white, 5 gray players
- Ball starts at the half way line with the white team who work the ball until they have the opportunity to play it forward.
- Players have to stay in their own area of the field (see cones)
- Play for about 5-10 minutes then change positions.
- Players can work on all types of turning and movement (Cruyff, drag back, etc,)

Coaching Points

- When to play
- Movement of the forwards.
- Movement off the ball
- Body position when receiving
- Be aware of the position of the defender, can you turn and face him or do you have to turn with him close to you.

Running with the Ball

Running with a ball is a natural thing, as a youngster you kick a ball and then run after it. If you wanted to move yourself quickly across the field with the ball you would use this skill. Zinedine Zidane is one of the best players in the world. It is exciting to watch him glide across the field with the ball. He is in full control but moves along effortlessly and at speed with the ball. Running with the ball is different to dribbling because you are not trying to beat defenders. You are just moving the ball from one part of the field to another.

The key factors for running with the ball are communication (before you receive the pass), good first touch, head up, body position and control of the ball while running.

The following chapter will introduce you to how to set up running with the ball sessions.

TRAINING SESSION 30:
Boxes and Balls

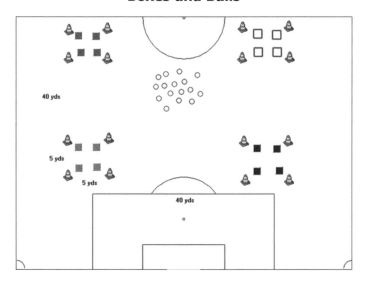

Setup

- ❂ 40 x 40 yds
- ❂ Boxes in each corner 5 x 5 yds
- ❂ 16 players can be used (4 teams of different colors each with their own box)
- ❂ Players try to collect as many balls as possible from the middle
- ❂ Once the balls are gone from the middle they can steal them from the corners
- ❂ All players start at their own box
- ❂ One player at all times must stay in the box
- ❂ 5-10 mins

Coaching Points

- ❂ Head up
- ❂ Good touch on the ball

TRAINING SESSION 31:
Tunnel Run #1

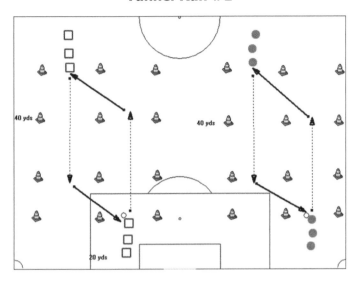

Setup

- ⊕ 20 x 40 yds (split into 10 x 40 channels)
- ⊕ 10 or more players
- ⊕ Players start running with the ball in the tunnel
- ⊕ 10 yds from the end they pass to the player facing on the opposite side of the tunnel

Coaching Points

- ⊕ First touch (out of the feet)
- ⊕ Body Position
- ⊕ Communication
- ⊕ Good pass
- ⊕ Get to the end as quickly as possible but with the ball under control

Variation

- ⊕ Change sides and use the left foot

TRAINING SESSION 32:
Tunnel Run #2

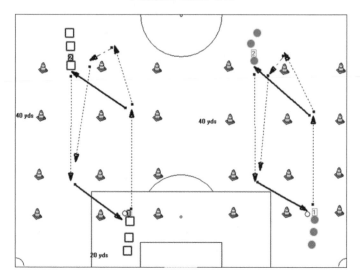

Setup

- ⊕ 20 x 40 yds (split into 10 x 40 channels)
- ⊕ 10 or more players
- ⊕ Players (position 1) start running with the ball in the tunnel
- ⊕ 10 yds from the end they pass to player 2 on the opposite side of the tunnel
- ⊕ After passing, player 1 chases after player 2 with the ball
- ⊕ The roles are reversed after the pass at the bottom

Coaching Points

- ⊕ First touch (out of the feet)
- ⊕ Body Position
- ⊕ Communication
- ⊕ Good pass
- ⊕ Get to the end as quickly as possible but with the ball under control

Variation

- ⊕ Change sides and use the left foot

TRAINING SESSION 33:
Running with the Ball in a Circle

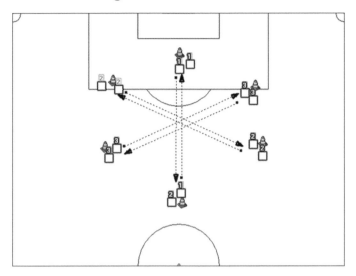

Setup

☺ Coned circle (size depending upon number of players)
☺ Players paired by the cones
☺ Players start by running with the ball through the circle
☺ When they are 10 feet away they pass to the next player
☺ 1's pass to 1's on the other side of the circle

Coaching Points

☺ First touch (out of the feet)
☺ Body Position
☺ Communication
☺ Good pass

TRAINING SESSION 34:
Four Corners

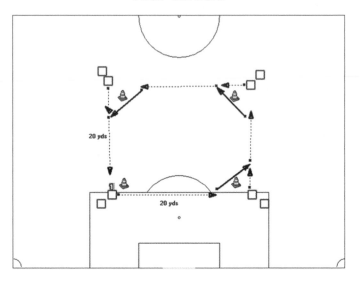

Setup

- 20 x 20
- 2 players in each corner
- Start at position 1
- Player runs with the ball and then passes the ball into the path of the other player before reaching the cone

Coaching Points

- First touch (out of the feet)
- Body Position
- Head up
- Control

Variation

- One-two pass with the player on the cone

TRAINING SESSION 35:
Breakout Game #1

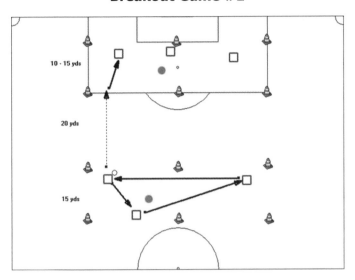

Setup

- ⊛ 8 players - 6 white, 2 gray
- ⊛ 3 v 1 in each box
- ⊛ After three passes the team with 3 recognizes the moment to run with the ball to the other box.
- ⊛ Once there, a pass is made before they enter the box

Coaching Points

- ⊛ First touch (out of the feet)
- ⊛ Body Position
- ⊛ Communication
- ⊛ Good pass
- ⊛ Recognize the moment to play

Variations

- ⊛ Change the number of passes
- ⊛ Smaller or larger area

TRAINING SESSION 36:
Breakout Game #2

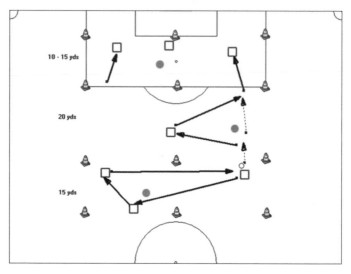

Setup

- 10 players - 7 white, 3 gray
- 3 v 1 in each box
- 1 v 1 in the middle area
- After three passes the team with 3 recognizes the moment to run with the ball to the other box.
- They can now play a one-two in the middle area

Coaching Points

- First touch (out of the feet)
- Body Position
- Communication
- Good pass
- Recognize the moment to play
- Movement of the middle area attacker

TRAINING SESSION 37:
Running with the Ball and Finishing with a Shot

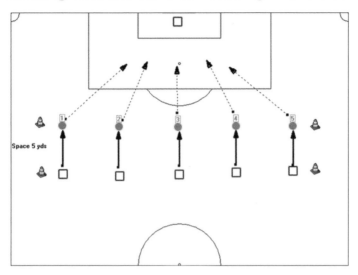

Setup

- ☻ 30 yds out from the goal
- ☻ 5 white (plus keeper) v 5 gray
- ☻ Space between defenders and attackers is 5 yds.
- ☻ Whites and grays pass to each other.
- ☻ When the coach shouts a number the gray players make the decision when they want to go
- ☻ They let the ball run through their legs and they are one on one with the keeper

Coaching Points

- ☻ Good passes
- ☻ Good first touch towards goal
- ☻ Head up (know where the keeper is)
- ☻ Good finish

Variation

- ☻ Allow the white team to chase after the grays and defend

TRAINING SESSION 38:
Running with the Ball - 6 v 6

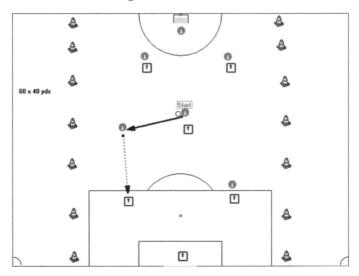

60 x 40 yds

Setup

⊛ 60 x 40 yds
⊛ 6 v 6
⊛ 2 goals
⊛ Start the game with a setup that encourages the players to run with the ball

Coaching Points

⊛ Encourage the players to run with the ball when the opportunity presents itself
⊛ First touch (out of the feet)
⊛ Body Position
⊛ Head up
⊛ Control

TRAINING SESSION 39:
Running with the Ball - 8 v 8

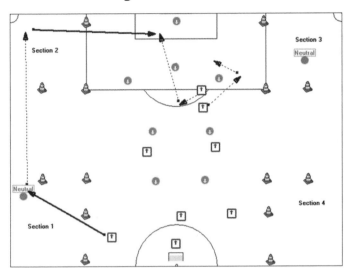

Setup

⚽ 8 white v 8 gray
⚽ 2 wingers playing for both teams
⚽ Wingers have to pick the ball up in one section and cross it in the other

Coaching Points

⚽ Good passes
⚽ Good first ball down the line
⚽ Head up so you can see the attackers before you cross
⚽ Movement of attackers
⚽ Good finish

Shooting

Shooting is one of the hardest skills to acquire and probably the most important. If you don't shoot you don't score goals, if you don't score goals you don't win games. Michael Owen, Thierry Henry and Ruud Van Nistelroy are all masters of shooting. They can shoot with either foot and look comfortable when they do it (most of the time). Players use different techniques to shoot, chipping, driving, passing are all types of shots. Many people seem to only remember the outstanding "rockets" scored from 30 yds but at the end of the match they all count as one goal.

The following points for the coach to observe are: players should accept responsibility of shooting (don't blame others if you miss), know where the keeper is before placement of the shot, technique of shooting (kicking foot and non-kicking foot and head). Is it the right time to shoot or pass. Accuracy comes before power.

The following chapter will introduce you to shooting.

TRAINING SESSION 40:
Shooting Warm Up

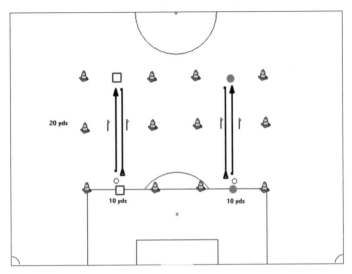

Setup

⊕ 10 x 20
⊕ Players begin by passing to each other through the gates
⊕ Can only score a goal if the pass goes through the gates
⊕ Play for 5-10 minutes

Coaching Points

⊕ Encourage the players to use the correct technique
⊕ Body Position
⊕ Angle of approach
⊕ Coach technique from different angles

Variations

⊕ Left and right foot
⊕ One touch/two touch

TRAINING SESSION 41:
1v1 Shooting

Setup

- Penalty area, players face the server
- Always start from the server (either pass with feet or throw over their heads)
- Play for 15-20 minutes

Coaching Points

- Be Alert
- Correct technique
- Movement of the players when they receive the ball

Variations

- One touch finish
- Make them sit down, lie down, jump before the ball is thrown
- Face away from the server

TRAINING SESSION 42:
2v2 Shooting

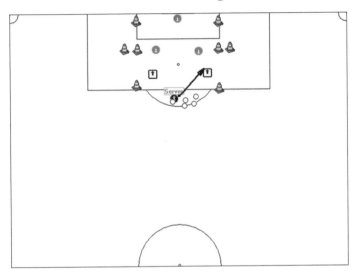

Setup

⊛ Penalty area, two cones are the offside line
⊛ 2 defenders and 2 attackers, a server and a goalkeeper
⊛ Always start from the server
⊛ Play for 15-20 minutes

Coaching Points

⊛ Creating space for the shot
⊛ Using opponents as screens to shoot past them
⊛ Fake and disguise your shots
⊛ Correct technique
⊛ Movement of the players
⊛ When to pass and when to shoot

Variations

⊛ One touch finish

TRAINING SESSION 43:
Running the Line

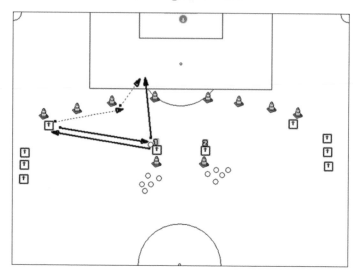

Setup

- ⊕ Half Field
- ⊕ 10-15 players
- ⊕ Start from 1 then after shot start from 2
- ⊕ 1 passes to the forward on the left who passes back and runs the line of the defense (cones)
- ⊕ Shooter switches sides after the shot

Coaching Points

- ⊕ Pass from the server and the forward
- ⊕ Run of the forward
- ⊕ When to pass
- ⊕ Movement of the forward
- ⊕ Type of shot

Variations

- ⊕ One touch finish
- ⊕ Add defenders in place of the cones

TRAINING SESSION 44:
2v2 Shooting with 2 Big Goals

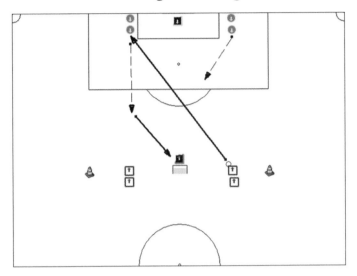

Setup

⊛ Make another penalty area (18 yds from the end of the other)
⊛ First player at the bottom passes diagonally to the first player
  at the top.
⊛ Teams switch ends after shot.

Coaching Points

⊛ Correct technique
⊛ Game speed
⊛ Movement of the players when they receive the ball
⊛ 2nd striker follows in on the shot.

Variations

⊛ One touch finish
⊛ Two touch finish
⊛ Variation of pass received (driven, chip, lofted etc)

TRAINING SESSION 45:
2v2v2 in the Box

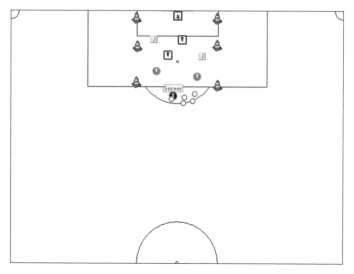

Setup

⊕ Penalty Area and two cones are the offside line
⊕ 3 teams of 2 players, a server and a goalkeeper
⊕ Always start from the server (server alternates passes)
⊕ Play for 15-20 minutes

Coaching Points

⊕ Creating space for the shot
⊕ Using opponents as screens to shoot past them
⊕ Fake shots
⊕ Correct technique
⊕ Movement of the players

Variations

⊕ One touch finish

TRAINING SESSION 46:
4v4 Shooting

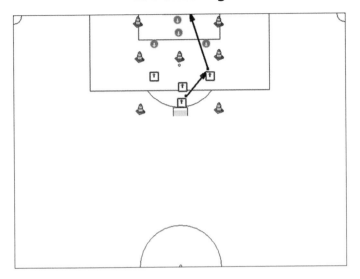

Setup

⊚ Penalty area divided into two halves
⊚ Teams are not allowed to go into the other half
⊚ 4 grays v 4 whites
⊚ Always start from the keeper
⊚ Play for 15-20 minutes

Coaching Points

⊚ Creating space for the shot
⊚ Using opponents as screens to shoot past them
⊚ Fake and disguise your shots
⊚ Correct technique
⊚ Movement of the players
⊚ When to pass and when to shoot

Variations

⊚ One touch finish

TRAINING SESSION 47:
Wide Angle Shooting

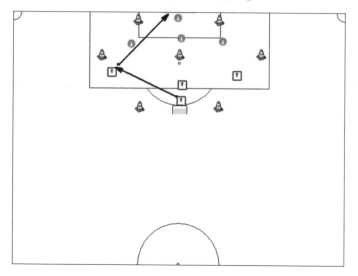

Setup

⊙ Penalty Area divided into two halves
⊙ Teams are not allowed to go into the other half
⊙ 4 grays v 4 whites
⊙ Always start from the keeper
⊙ Play for 15-20 minutes

Coaching Points

⊙ Creating space for the shot
⊙ Encourage your players to shoot from angles
⊙ Shooting from angles, shoot across the keeper
⊙ Correct technique
⊙ Movement of the players
⊙ When to pass and when to shoot

Variations

⊙ One touch finish

TRAINING SESSION 48:
Layoff and Shot

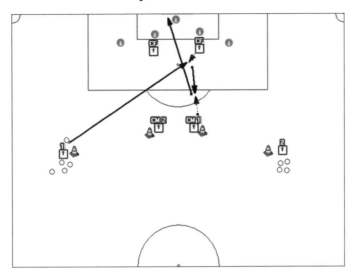

Setup

⊛ In and around the penalty area
⊛ 6 attackers (white) and 4 defenders (gray)
⊛ Sever 1 passes the ball in to the center forward (CF)
⊛ CF lays the ball back on the edge of the box for the center midfielder (CM) to shoot

Coaching Points

⊛ Pass from the server
⊛ Movement of the forwards (make space away from the defender and come to the ball)
⊛ Layoff pass should be cushioned and the CM's should be able to strike without having to control
⊛ Movement of CM's and shooting technique

Variations

⊛ Add more defenders and attackers
⊛ Add more servers
⊛ Allow forwards to score without having to lay it back

TRAINING SESSION 49:
9v9 Shooting Drill

Setup

⊛ 3 areas, 10 x 30 yds
⊛ Teams are not allowed to go into the other areas
⊛ Always start from the keeper
⊛ Play for 15-20 minutes

Coaching Points

⊛ Creating space for the shot
⊛ Correct technique
⊛ Movement of the players
⊛ When to pass and when to shoot

Variations

⊛ One touch finish
⊛ Can only score from headers and volleys

Defending

The art of defending is a vital skill. Over the years we have seen very creative defenders emerge, Franco Baresi, Bobby Moore, Alan Hansen to name a few. Defenders are not just there to defend, we need to coach our defenders to be comfortable on the ball and become attack minded when they have the opportunity.

The key factors for defending are watch the opponent, make up the ground while the ball is traveling, watch the ball, be patient, select the right time to tackle and intercept the ball if you can.

The following chapter will introduce you to how to set up a defending session.

TRAINING SESSION 50:
Defending Warm Up

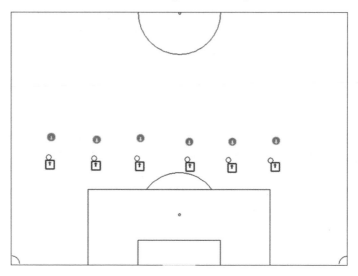

Setup

- ☺ White players slowly dribble the ball to the half way line, gray players jog backwards defending and jockeying.
- ☺ At the halfway line, gray takes the ball and dribbles back with white defending
- ☺ Attack the defender right and left, make the defenders show the attacker one way.
- ☺ Lead foot should stay balanced

Coaching Points

- ☺ Slowly to begin and then step up the pace.
- ☺ Make sure the defender is balanced and is showing the attacker one way.

TRAINING SESSION 51:
Which Side of the Ball to Defend #1

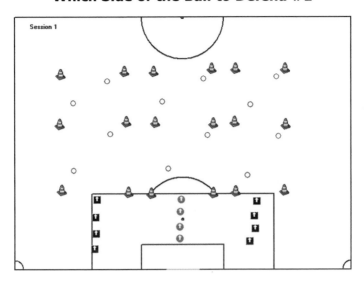

Setup

- ⊛ 10 x 20
- ⊛ 3 teams of 4, 12 balls
- ⊛ On the coach's command the first player goes
- ⊛ Make the player defend the ball in the correct way.
- ⊛ One at a time to begin, then in pairs, and eventually fours.
- ⊛ On the next shout, the next player goes; eventually you will have 4 players on all the balls (see session 2)

Coaching Points

- ⊛ Leading foot, show the attacker one way to the line.
- ⊛ Make sure the defenders are not too close to the ball, flat footed, or on their back foot.

TRAINING SESSION 52:
Which Side of the Ball to Defend #2

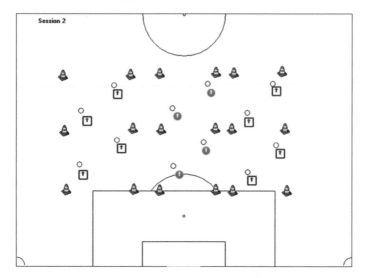

TRAINING SESSION 53:
Defending the Pass 2v1 #1

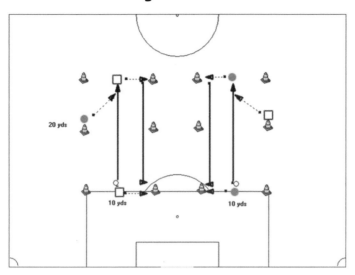

Setup

- ☺ 10 x 20 yds
- ☺ 2 v1
- ☺ The ball starts with either player at the end line
- ☺ When the player receives the ball the defender (player at the side) can defend the ball
- ☺ Players at either end are not allowed to come off their line but they can move from side to side

Coaching Points

- ☺ Can the defender intercept?
- ☺ Angle of approach
- ☺ Movement of the defender as the ball travels

Variations

- ☺ Let the defender move when the ball is played
- ☺ Allow the attackers to come off the line and attack the defender
- ☺ Add another defender (see session 2)

TRAINING SESSION 54:
Defending the Pass 2v1 #2

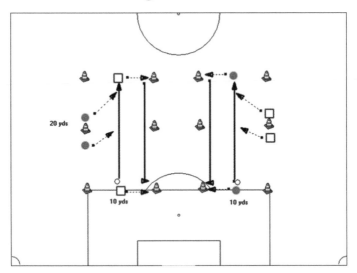

Same as session #1 but with an extra defender.

TRAINING SESSION 55:
Covering and Defending 2v2

Setup

⊛ 10 x 10 yds
⊛ 2 v2
⊛ White passes the ball to the Gray team.
⊛ The Gray team has to pass it between or to the White team behind to score a goal
⊛ Start with a diagonal pass
⊛ Make it match related, offside, tackling etc.

Coaching Points

⊛ Closest player adds pressure, first player covers the player with the ball
⊛ Second player covers and third and fourth.
⊛ If the attackers switch the ball, the defenders switch
⊛ Stay inside your own box 2 gray and 2 white

TRAINING SESSION 56:
Defending 4v2

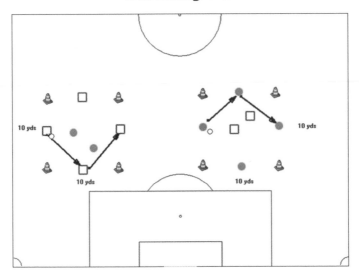

Setup

- ⊕ 10 x 10 yds
- ⊕ 4 v2
- ⊕ Teams with 4 have to keep possession of the ball
- ⊕ Teams of 4 are not allowed inside the square, teams inside the square are not allowed out

Coaching Points

- ⊕ The two in the middle have to work as a team
- ⊕ First player marks the player with the ball, second player covers
- ⊕ Communication

TRAINING SESSION 57:
Defending 4v4

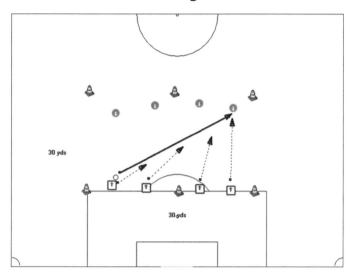

Setup

- 30 x 30 yds
- Diagonal pass to the opposing team
- The back four have to defend as a team.
- Play with offside and make it match related
- To score a goal get to the white or gray teams line with the ball

Coaching Points

- Coach the four as a unit on how to defend, cover & balance.
- Shape like a dish and a wave.
- Make sure the defenders move from side to side when the ball is switched
- Easiest and simplest exercise on how to coach a defending four

TRAINING SESSION 58:
Fussball

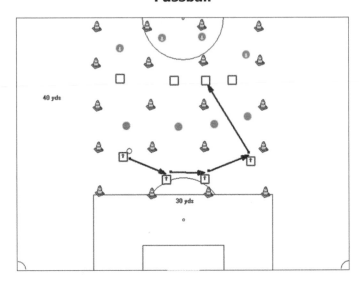

Setup

- 30 x 40
- 16 players (8 gray and 8 white)
- Teams are not allowed to leave the boxed area 30 x 10
- Teams try to work the ball side to side and get it to the other white team
- Gray team has to defend them
- If the gray team gains possession they try to get it to the other gray team
- They get 1 point if they succeed.

Coaching Points

- The four defenders have to work as a team
- Balancing and covering
- Nearest player has to close the ball, the other three provide cover

Variation

- Change the area if the players struggle (make it smaller)
- You can add more players and make the area bigger.

TRAINING SESSION 59:
Exercise to Improve Covering and Defending

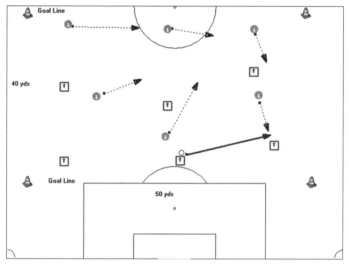

Setup

⊛ 40 x 50 yds
⊛ 6 whites v 6 grays play a proper game, score a goal by getting it over the goal line.

Coaching Points

⊛ Explain and show the players correct body posture and position in relation to the ball and their team mates.
⊛ Defend in numbers and as a team.
⊛ Make sure players get to the correct side of the ball, defend as a team.
⊛ Make sure the team shift as a team when the ball gets switched.
⊛ Make sure the players understand the importance of seeing the man and the ball.
⊛ Don't let anyone in behind you.

TRAINING SESSION 60:
Defending as a Team #1

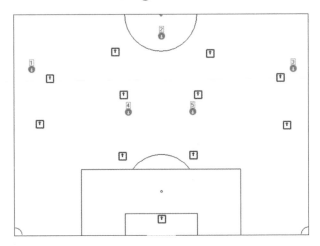

Setup

- ⊕ Half Field
- ⊕ 11 v 5
- ⊕ Coach shouts a gray player's number, the team defends as if that player has possession.
- ⊕ The attacking team all have a number and a ball.

Coaching Points

- ⊕ Make the team shift as a team, watch for lazy players who go through the motions.
- ⊕ Has to become second nature, get the players to imagine they are all tied together
- ⊕ Once one pulls one way the others follow (see session 2).
- ⊕ Make sure your keeper is in the right place
- ⊕ Team shape when defending (see session 2)

Variation

- ⊕ Let the gray team attack once the white team is used to defending and covering
- ⊕ This time when you shout a number the other four leave their balls and attack with the number called

TRAINING SESSION 61:
Defending as a Team #2

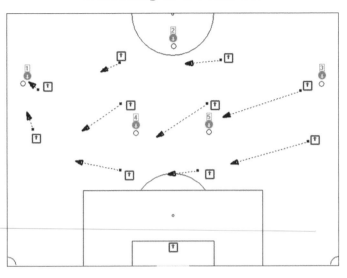

⊙ If the coach shouts number 1 the team reacts accordingly
⊙ The whole team moves as a team

TRAINING SESSION 62:
Turn Defending into an Attack

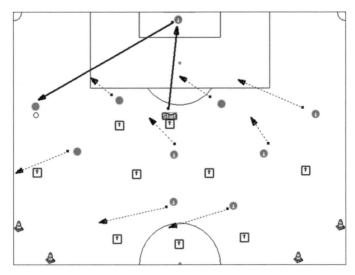

Setup

- ⊛ Half Field
- ⊛ 10 v 9
- ⊛ Two coned goals for the gray (defending team) to score in
- ⊛ Start with the white team (see starting white player)
- ⊛ White player strikes the ball to the keeper and we play from there

Coaching Points

- ⊛ Turn defense into attack quickly
- ⊛ If the pass is on can we execute it?
- ⊛ Team needs to shift and pass the ball

Variations

- ⊛ Play open play after 5 - 10 mins
- ⊛ Play to a goal and then the team who concedes starts the game (either from half way line or goal kick)
- ⊛ Use a goal on the half way line and take away the cones

Crossing and Finishing

When you watch soccer teams attack they attack in two areas of the field. They either attack on the wings or down the middle. From Johan Cruyff to David Beckham we have seen talented wide midfielders tease and deliver pinpoint crosses. Place Pele or Alan Shearer on the end of their crosses and you only have one outcome: **Goooooooooal!**

Important key factors to remember when coaching crossing and finishing are space available (do the players have enough space to deliver a cross?), the position of the defenders, the position of the attackers and the technique required in executing the cross or finishing.

Key Factors for the coach:

Crossing

- Position of the ball before delivery
- Place of contact on the ball
- Is the delivery accurate?

Finishing from the cross

- Angle of the run
- Timing
- Get in front of the defender
- Disguise the run
- Contact on the ball to finish

The following chapter will introduce you to crossing and finishing.

TRAINING SESSION 63:
Finishing Warm Up #1

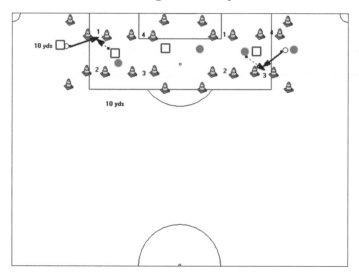

Setup

- ⊛ Grids 10 x 10 yds.
- ⊛ 4 players in each grid (3 attackers and 1 defender).
- ⊛ Ball is passed using the hands.
- ⊛ Lose your man and get between the gates numbered 1, 2, 3 & 4 to score a goal
- ⊛ You can only receive the pass and score a goal between the gates (numbered 1-4)
- ⊛ You can't carry the ball into the gate.
- ⊛ You have to be standing between the gates when you receive the ball to score.
- ⊛ Once they score a goal the ball is passed to the opposite side of the grid.
- ⊛ Play for 5 mins then change.

Coaching Points

- ⊛ Show the players how to lose a defender
- ⊛ You are working on body position and communication
- ⊛ Keep the players moving.

TRAINING SESSION 64:
Finishing Warm Up #2

Setup

◉ 10 x 10 yds
◉ 4 players to each grid.
◉ Side foot pass to begin with, one touch, two touch

Variations

◉ Players pick the ball up and throw it to the other player; they then hit a half volley to the other player.
◉ Pass forward then lay it back then pass forward again.
◉ Step in front of the cone and hit the ball.
◉ Change the angle of approach.

TRAINING SESSION 65:
Crossing Warm Up

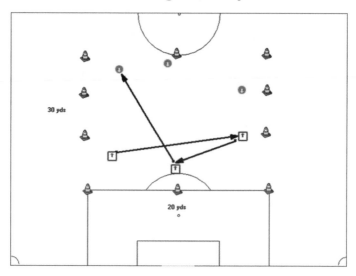

Setup

- 30 x 20
- 3 Gray, 3 White
- Pass between the three and then cross the ball to the other team
- Repeat
- 10 mins

Coaching Points

- Movement
- Correct crossing technique

TRAINING SESSION 66:
Movement of Forwards in the Box

Setup

⚽ Half Field
⚽ 1 attacker, 2 servers (1 & 2) and1 goalkeeper
⚽ Place 4 cones in the area.
⚽ Make the attacker use the movements around the cones shown at the bottom of the diagram.

Coaching Points

⚽ Timing of runs
⚽ No standing in the box (easy to mark)
⚽ Pick out runners from the server
⚽ Early Cross

TRAINING SESSION 67:
Crossing and Finishing Game

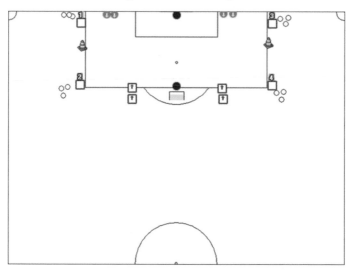

Setup

- Penalty Box
- 12 (white and gray) players and 2 goalkeepers (black) plus 2 goals
- 1 player on each corner of the penalty box
- Numbers 2 and 4 deliver the ball to the white team
- Numbers 1 and 3 deliver the ball to gray team

Coaching Points

- Timing of the runs
- Delivery of the cross
- Movement of the forwards
- Position of the cross

Variation

- One touch cross from where the servers stand
- Two touch cross, deliver when you get to the cone or when you get to the byline

TRAINING SESSION 68:
2v1 Attacking Wing Play

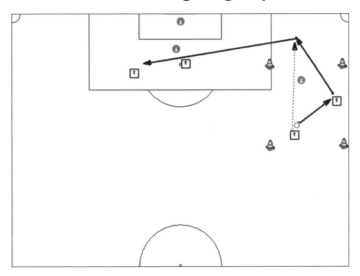

Setup

- ☉ Half Field
- ☉ 4 attackers 2 defenders and a goalkeeper.
- ☉ Encourage 2 v 1
- ☉ Play quick and pass and move
- ☉ Play offside

Coaching Points

- ☉ Coach the attackers on their movement
- ☉ Coach wide midfielders and full backs on how to link up
- ☉ Communication
- ☉ When is the cross coming?

TRAINING SESSION 69:
Switching Play and Attacking Down the Wings

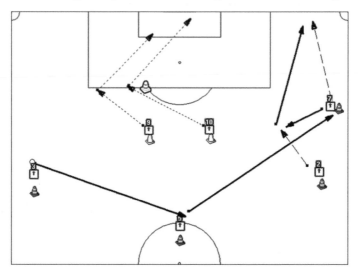

Setup

⊕ Half Field
⊕ Ball starts with the left back (3) who pulls it back to the center back (5)
⊕ Center back switches out wide to the right mid fielder (7)
⊕ Right back (2) makes a run forward, right mid (7) drops it back
⊕ Right back (2) puts the right mid (7) in the corner to make a cross
⊕ 2 forwards (9 & 10) on the cone make arced runs into the box, one near, one far post

Coaching Points

⊕ Play at game pace, switch play with crisp passes
⊕ Good passes and movement
⊕ Variation
⊕ Add more players, end up with an 8 v 8
⊕ Change sides
⊕ End with a game at match pace.

TRAINING SESSION 70:
Movement of the Forwards and the Center Midfielder

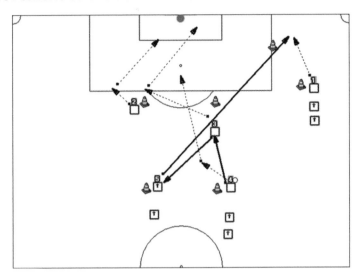

Setup

⊛ Half Field
⊛ 5 stations
⊛ Ball starts at station 4
⊛ Player 4 plays to 3 who checks off the cone, 3 plays to 5, 5 plays into the corner for 1 who crosses
⊛ Only score from a cross to begin
⊛ Play for 15-20 minutes

Coaching Points

⊛ Timing of the forwards and the center midfielder
⊛ Position of the cross
⊛ Pass and move

Variation

⊛ Add defenders and turn it into a game
⊛ Play from both sides

TRAINING SESSION 71:
Attacking Down the Wings 9v9

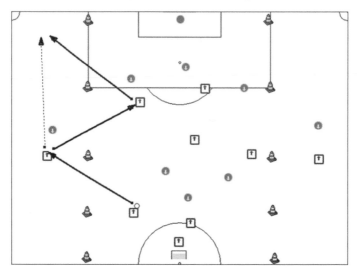

Setup

⊕ Half Field
⊕ 9 v 9
⊕ 7 v 7 in the middle area 1 v 1 on the outside
⊕ Only one player from each team in the outside channels
⊕ Only score from a cross to begin
⊕ Play for 15-20 minutes

Coaching Points

⊕ Timing of the forwards
⊕ Position of the cross
⊕ Pass and move

Variation

⊕ Allow another attacker into the channels to create 2 v 1
⊕ Encourage overlapping, if you pass into the channels you have to overlap and cross then you stay in there and the other player comes out

TRAINING SESSION 72:
Crossing Corners Game

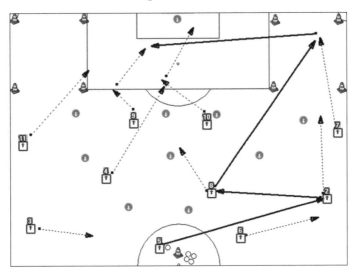

Setup

- Half Field
- 10 blue and 9 red
- Half Field (4, 10 x 10 coned areas)
- Can only score from a cross to begin with and only a cross from within the boxes
- Always start from the half way line
- Play for 15-20 minutes

Coaching Points

- Encourage the team to move the ball side to side until options open up
- Coach crosses from all 4 areas, different types of crosses
- Try to bring the red team out and then get in behind them
- Movement of all players
- Position of the cross
- Pass and move

Goalkeeping

Goalkeepers are the last line of defense and the first line of attack. At times it can be the loneliest position on the field. Make a mistake and everyone will remember, make a great save and you are just doing your job. Over the years we have seen some great keepers, Dino Zoff, Peter Schmeichel, Peter Shilton and Gordon Banks. Goalkeeping is an art form which needs to be coached. Realizing this, it is very surprising that many coaches neglect their goalkeeper during soccer coaching sessions.

The following chapter will introduce you to a collection of goalkeeping sessions.

TRAINING SESSION 73:
Goalkeeping Warm Up

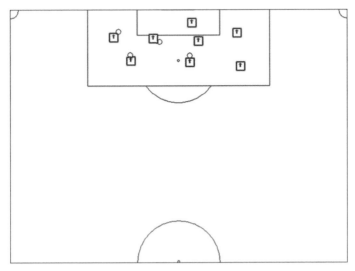

Setup

⚽ 8 Keepers (4 with balls, 4 without)
⚽ Move around and throw the ball to each other

Coaching Points

⚽ Correct catching technique
⚽ Correct throwing technique
⚽ Eye hand coordination
⚽ Movement of keepers to the ball

Variation

⚽ Half volley pass
⚽ Roll the ball

TRAINING SESSION 74:
Goalkeeping Footwork

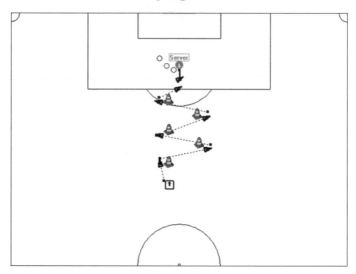

Setup

- One server and a keeper (add more servers if you have more keepers)
- Goalkeeper weaves in and out of the cones
- Once through, the server throws them a ball to save

Coaching Points

- Quick feet
- Be ready for the shot at the end

Variation

- Add more cones
- Add different obstacles

TRAINING SESSION 75:
Shot Stopping

Setup

- ✪ 12 yd wide goal (use portable goal or flags)
- ✪ 1 keeper 2 servers
- ✪ Server 1 takes a shot
- ✪ Goalkeeper makes a save and then immediately gets up and turns around ready for the shot off server 2

Coaching Point

- ✪ Keeper should recover quickly
- ✪ Be alert

Variations

- ✪ Reduce or increase size of goal
- ✪ Add a a player to follow in on the shot
- ✪ Make the keeper start at the post/flag

TRAINING SESSION 76:
Shots on Goal

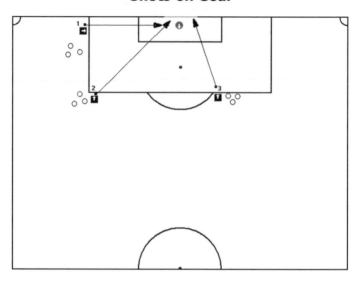

Setup

⊕ In and around the penalty area
⊕ 3 servers and a goalkeeper
⊕ Server 1 crosses hard and low
⊕ Server 2 shoots for one side of the goal
⊕ Server 3 shoots for the other side of the goal

Coaching Points

⊕ Keeper should be ready and on his toes
⊕ Movement before and after shot
⊕ Position before shot
⊕ Steady and ready for shot

Variation

⊕ Change order of shot
⊕ Change type of shot
⊕ Add an attacker for rebounds

TRAINING SESSION 77:
Angled Shot Stopping

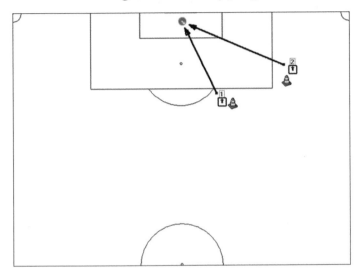

Setup

⊙ In and around the penalty area
⊙ 2 Servers and 1 Keeper

Coaching Points

⊙ Movement into the line
⊙ Movement down the line
⊙ Set yourself before the shot
⊙ Decision process

Variation

⊙ Server 1 strikes, then server 2
⊙ Server 1 passes to server 2 who shoots
⊙ Add an attacker for rebounds
⊙ Add a defender

TRAINING SESSION 78:
Three Sided Goal

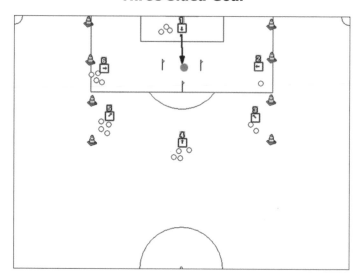

Setup

⚽ 30 yds long and width of penalty area
⚽ Coach calls a server number and the server tries to score
⚽ Goalkeeper must move quickly around the flags

Coaching Points

⚽ Movement of keeper between shots
⚽ Save technique
⚽ Speed of recovery

Variation

⚽ Add defenders (use only one ball)

TRAINING SESSION 79:
4v4 Small Sided Game

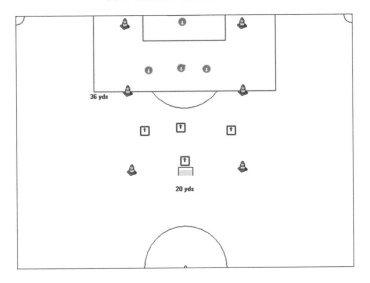

Setup

⚽ 36 yds long (2 penalty areas) and 20 yds wide
⚽ 4 v 4
⚽ Start at the keepers

Coaching Points

⚽ Communication from the keeper
⚽ Angles
⚽ Shot stopping and technique
⚽ Distribution from the keeper

TRAINING SESSION 80:
Goalkeeper Pressure Drill

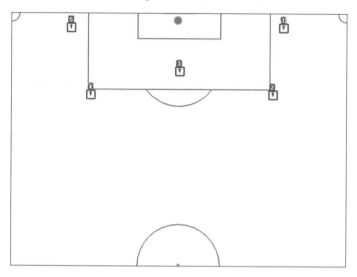

Setup

- 1 goalkeeper and 5 servers with balls
- Coach shouts a number and that server strikes a ball at the keeper
- Each server has a different type of shot to hit (chip, driven high, lofted, in swinging, driven low)

Coaching Points

- Position of the keeper before the shot
- Movement of the keeper
- Adjustment of the keeper after the shot
- Recovery rate

Variation

- Add attackers and defenders to distract the keeper

TRAINING SESSION 81:
Dealing with Crosses to the Far Post

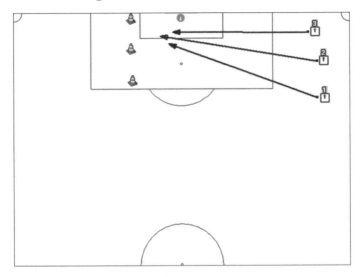

Setup

⊛ Cone off part of the area (not in use)
⊛ Different types of delivery (in swinging and out swinging)
⊛ Coach calls a server number (keeper has to adjust position)

Coaching Points

⊛ Starting position of the keeper depends upon the type of delivery
⊛ Assess the area and ball trajectory
⊛ Decision to come or not to come
⊛ Angle of approach, timing, catch or punch, placement of clearance

Variation

⊛ Add defenders
⊛ Add attackers

TRAINING SESSION 82:
Cross and Distribution

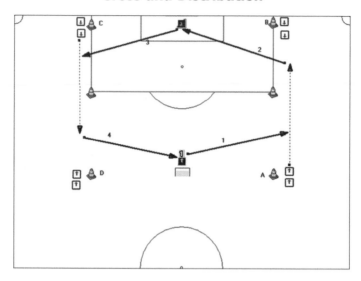

Setup

- ❂ 36 yd x width of the penalty area
- ❂ 2 keepers and 8-12 players
- ❂ Ball starts with the keeper
- ❂ Keeper throws it to the advancing player on the right
- ❂ Player dribbles down the field and crosses it to the other keeper
- ❂ Keeper gathers and distributes

Coaching Point

- ❂ Position of the keeper before the cross
- ❂ Transition speed between catching the ball and releasing the ball

Variations

- ❂ Allow the winger to cut in and shoot
- ❂ Add attackers and defenders